W0259447

The Lillian Lectures

a book by

Doctor Mildred Undertwang

drawings by Flint Geinsburger

Coach House Books

First Edition

Authorized for use in Ontario Schools.

CANADIAN CATALOGUING IN PUBLICATION DATA

Agnew, Wendy, 1951-
The Lillian Lectures

Series of performance pieces.
ISBN 1-55245-015-5

I. Title.

PS8551.G635L54 1999 C812'.54 C98-931115-5
PR9199.3.A36L54 1999

Dedicated to the kids

Playhouse

#16a

Sally Ashton
has a very big bum
It's good,
she uses it as a cushion
for her whole family to cluster on
when they're sad
She bounces them on it
and they laugh
Once her brother Avery
fell down the crack
and didn't come out for days
Finally they had to
put sugar on her tongue
and he crawled out her nostril
with stories of the inside

He said it was just like the Ex,
except wetter

#16b

One thing Avery saw
was frogs on her heart
Their little platypus fingers
pushing into the red
making it beat
all talking
about being princes
and kissing each other
with red
froggy lips

#16c

The king frog
can never become a prince
but only has a golden crown
and manages the other frogs

He sits on
the biggest heart in the world
all day long
and thinks about Jupiter
the planet of wisdom
and catches cupids
with his tongue

Then they have to tell him
about love so he can coach the princes

He was on Mother Theresa's heart for a while
but he got tired
of the salt sea surrounding it
so he left

O.K. Lillian Pillian Rillian
listen to this:

Mothers and fathers have
a pact with the devil
when they decide not to become nuns
but to get married and have sex
because that's where we get babies
The devil makes the man swallow a frog
on their wedding night
that's why your father burps sometimes
and the woman has to swallow a spider
Then the frog and the spider crawl out
and look at them when they're sleeping
and see what they look like
then the frog spits on some dust
and the spider weaves the dust and spit
into a baby that sorta looks
like your mom and dad
then the spider drags it back inside
the mommie's tummy
That's how you got born
Pretty neat eh?

Now the baby grows inside there
'cause your mom catches flies
and eats them at night
when nobody can see her
OK that's why mothers always swat flies
in the day time
to build up a supply
so the spider keeps weaving the baby
and when the baby comes out
there's this cord on it from the web
and when they cut the cord
the poor spider dies
When I have a baby
I'm going to keep eating lots of flies
after the baby's born
so my spider can
still live

#4a

Geese have long necks

why?

'cause they
are God's spies
and they look up
nuns' dresses
That's why Mother Goose
has all those stories
'cause up nuns' dresses
is where all
the best stories are

#4b

Once

a goose
went right up
a nun's hole
and into her universe
and sprouted wings
and flew
and that's
what a crow is
a renegade nun
with a
goose in her

#8

John Hislop
lost his dink

why?

Because his mom
didn't know nothin'
about sex
because she was a nun before
so when John was born
she said "O my God
that child's got a thumb
coming out of his petunia
it must be
the devil's hand"
and she grabbed it
trying to pull out
the devil
and ripped it
clean off

#0

My mother's belly was stuffed
with dandelion fluff
And when I was born
a million million parachutes
spewmed out of her and on each chute
there was a idea

And whenever I get a idea
that chute sticks onto me
so when all the ideas are got by me
then I float up to heaven

#7

If you want a boy to love you
get his toenail
and if you can
some of his snot
put them in a sock
and bury it under your parents' mattress
when you know they're gonna be doing it
listen for the creakings
and when you hear them going at it
spin around three times outside their door
whispering
love me love me love me
then you gotta spit
and make a cross on their door with bitsy juice
and then at breakfast
you gotta say the boy's name three times
without anyone noticing
like if it's Harry you can say
"that's a harry looking peach"
or if it's Dean you can say
"she'll be a deanager in a while"
pretending you have a cold
the boy will love you
and don't fall in love with him

the way not to
is to put a bean in your belly button
'cause that's where
the boy's love seed
goes in

#15

Sandra Ribonski is my friend
She collects stones
and then we lie down
and put them on each other
and imagine we're mother earth
and then we have an earthquake

Sometimes
we put a whole bunch of them
into our mouths and sing
O Canada
and sometimes we kiss
and pass one stone
into each other's mouths
and pretend it's our boyfriend
and the stone is the baby seed
and then we lie down
and scream and scream and
have a baby
and then we have a funeral
because the baby died
We got little crosses
all over the field
and then we make up a song
about misery

#1

When a baby's born
there's a cord stuck onto its thing
and the cord goes
thru the mother
and is hooked onto God's tonsil
and when the baby comes out
and the cord breaks
God's tonsil goes a wigglin'
and a wigglin'
and he makes a song
and that's the wind

School

#18

Norbert Schmidt is a German
His dad was a Nazi in WWII
and killed a bunch of people
with pills that turned into bad air

Norbert says
all those dead people
come into his room at night
and it's so crowded
he can hardly breathe
and he has to sing them lullabies till dawn
for them to go away

Norbert's mother drinks beer
and sings Santa Lucia
in the back yard
and his father is in prison somewhere

She feels bad she chose
such a loser for a husband
so she's making a new one
out of lint from the dryer

She's naming him Puffy
and she's making him have
no arms and no mouth

HELLO

why do we say that?

Hello... hello...

because devils can't stand circles
so when you say hello to someone
you lure out the devils
by calling the name of their home
and then you nail 'em
with a circle
Hell .... O
Hell .... O
Hell .... O!

It's scary eh?

Once Andrea Phipps
was playing the see-how-long-
you-can-leave-off-the-O game
and she choked on a bee
so she never could say the O
and the devils took away her brain
that's why she flunked grade two

Poor kid
all she had to do was make the O
with her hand
and she would have been saved

HELL................

So

why can't devils stand circles?

'cause
a long time ago
the angels got halos
on their heads
to keep their brains from growing
bigger than God's
but some angels
are letting their brains grow
anyway
and the halos
cut into their brains
and made them crabby
and that's
a devil

#13a

O.K.   Masturbate
What's it mean?

C'mon Lillian
What's it mean?

Just take a guess

No no no no no no
no no no no no no
NO!

Boy are you dumb!
        It means this...

touch your thing

go on
        won't bite ya

O.K. now rub up and down...
O.K. Stop

Now I'm going to do it
        no I'm not

Because you know why
because in the olden days
in the olden days, Lillian
when there were dragons
and flying monsters
and horrible goblins.
That thing you just did
That was the way
you called up those things
the magic way
Sometimes witches would even stick brooms
covered with magic soup
up their things
        Yep... that's how...
why even today
you can call them up
but you only get their ghosts
because they all died
after God was invented   Sooo
it's even worse now
because you can't see them
you can't even see them

That's why they changed
the name to masturbates

because they couldn't bear
the thought of those slimy spectres
those gigantic hags
those evil evil forces
hangin' around

        Monsterbaiting is what it
really is
        monsterbaiting... and you
just did it

        Shhhh...
d'you hear something scratching?

BLAGGGHH!!!

#14a

Angels don't have fun
'cause they're always praying
and crows have lots of fun
but they get shot at

they get to eat road kill
and fly south
for the winter

one angel
collected crow feathers
and made herself
a secret wing
all black
and she'd fly down
and play with the crows
till God
caught her by the toe
held her upside down
and hung her off a tree

the crows saw
she had no bitsy
and pecked out her eyes

#14b

Crows got a terror of angels
sometimes that's why
they go south
for the winter

'cause all that snow
reminds them of heaven
and how black they are
and how mean
God is

#14c

God's not always mean
He saves the sparrows
but crows are too big and noisy
God only likes lambs and kittens and donkeys
– anything weak or stupid –
'cause He's not too bright Hisself
otherwise why would He hang out
with a bunch of angels
in a land where
there's nothing but air

#13b

Lillian told me
my soul was in her pencil case

She captured it
when I was monster baiting

She says if i don't be good
she'll cut off my dink
and fill it with ink
and it will write swears
by itself on the walls of our house
and all the bad things
it will write too and then
my dink will go crazy
and hunt me down
and kill me
by peeing me with ink
till I drown

that's why
I'm taking
swimming lessons

#133

Andrea Phipps got sent to the Cath licken school
God's breedin farm
she saw a sad guy nailded to a plus sign
and studied real hard
she got a A in math
'cause she didn't want that happening to her

#21

Samuel Struntz is the boy I love
He sits at the desk in front of me
and when he's not looking
I show him my tits

The tit fairies zoom out
and stick to his hair
and crawl in his ears
and tell him how beautiful I am

Soon he will be smitten
within an inch of his life!

#48

Arzoom Alumium gived the teacher a apple
sayin' all girl teachers come from the devil
cause they made Adam
bite on the fruit o' knowledge
and he choked

Mr. Phipps can make his tie jump
by wibble-wobblin' his throat apple
urp urp urp urp urp

If there's a magic apple in everyone's throat
there must be a trap door
keeping it from falling into the stomach

if they could only find the key to the door
they'd be smart as God

The girl teachers hide the keys
under their tongues
that's why they're always going   *tsk tsk*

they like to suck
on the taste
of the gold

#3f

Sueanne Zefler says
It's not Tinkerbell
It's **Dink**erbell

That's why all the men
have to get circumsized
because their scrotums dont ring
unless their dink looks like a bell

She says if your dink
looks like a sausage
your scrotum just goes
thunk thunk

Peter Pan is a story
about a boy getting circumsized
into a man

Do you believe
in fairies?

#101

Mary Magdalene had a baby girl
that was Queen Elizabeth
who invented the Spanish Armada
and Christopher Columbus

Christopher Columbus was slow
so Queen Elizabeth told him to peel apples
and then he invented gravity

Meanwhile the Indians looked in their crystal ball
and saw that all Europeans were mad
because of rats
and so they sent them a potion
but it backfired
and the Indians and Queen Elizabeth fought

She was insulted
so that's why Zeus chopped North America
off from Europe

Christopher Columbus got cooked
and eaten by cannibals
and Queen Elizabeth married Sitting Bull
and they had Pierre Trudeau as a baby
and then they died

'cause the ghost of Christopher Columbus
came back as George Armstrong Custer
and chopped off both their heads

The End

Culvert

#77

If a guy is walking down the street
and horks never look

Otherwise the cooties will crawl up
your eye beams
infecting your brain with grunt words

And when someone says
"How are you little girl?"
Your head will spin around three times
and you'll yell "Fuck you and all your family
bastard nose weeds!"

And then you'll have to be sent to live in a culvert
by the dump and eat dead sea gulls and
poor people church cookies
from Brenda Wallhoosier's
mom

Why do apples be so bad?

Cut a apple open sideways
what do ya get?

A star

What's a star?

Mary Magdalene's cunt
which is where
God's brain is hid

Do you like me?
I like you...

So
when Eve bit the apple
God got pissed off
cause she was chewing on his brain
AND
Mary Magdalene's cunt.

#34

Lucy Lafrinsky says her vulva can fly

It unglues itself
from her body
when her mother
closes the door

It slips through the crack
and it drinks the light
out of the lamps
at nightime

That's where dreams come from

#32

Daddies' got a frog tongue
underneath their belly button
when the moon is full
they zap it up there
and all the unborn babies
climb down it

Then every Tuesday
your dad goes to work
and catapolts the babies
into the air

some go splat on the windows
but some o' them
get sucked down chimleys
and then your mom breathes them in

Then they got to spend nine whole months
finding the key to the belly button door
so they can get out
and start ramming around
as kids

The key is hidden
in one of your mom's teeth

#33

That's what dentists do
they put belly button keys
in your mom's teeth

In your dad
they put car keys

#36

Mothers got breasts

            ya know why?

'cause a human baby
tries to push it's way out the chest first
and it keeps rammin' its head
from the inside
(till dents form)

finally it tires
and swims down to the vajina

by then
the horns are all thunked off

I wish I was a rhino
they go out the right hole
first time

#312

white lines
on the highway

skidmarks
of angels

#20

The sun is God's bellybutton
if you stare too hard at it
you might get sucked into Her tummy
'cause She's a girl!
And then there you'd be,
Lillian
swimming around in all those unborn babies
and you could teach them
about life on the outside
and get them to swear allegiance
like to the flag
and then you could muster them
onto sunbeams
and float down the biblicles to earth
and become the queen
of everything

#20b

God is a morphrodite
...both boy and girl at the same time...
like a worm

that's what halos are
golden God worms making love
to themselves

Third Cubicle

#2

Cicely Mulgridge put a apple up her bum
Now the tree of knowlege
is growing up inside her
that's why she's sprouting bumps on her chetsts
and that's why they're called
chetstsnuts

At Christmastime her dad will hack them off
and pop them in the fire place
then Jesus will come out
and fly around the christmas tree
chasin' the tooth fairy for her money

She hides on the top
till God comes down the chimley
dressed in his wife Jill's red bathrobe
God hatches the chetstsnuts into God popcorn
which is gifts

But Jesus just wants to bang the tooth fairy
and get her money
that's why God gives the gifts
to the other children
and Jesus has to fight
the devil on halloween

#3

Fuck is a bad word.
If you see kay
tell her her underwear
is showing

All boys got a sausage

If you see kay
tell her that poop is a baby
that said
If you see kay
to God before they got bornded

Not born babies
gotta mind their pees and clues

If you see kay tell her
I've gone to look at
Jimmy Zofler's sausage
for an nickle

that's **If you see kay**

fart!

#4

when a baby's sleepin' inside the mother
if it wakes up and bangs its head
on the roof of her
it might say
If you see Kay
an' that's O.K.

But if God wakes the baby up
to teach it about angels
and the baby says
"Fuck off old man, I'm sleepin' here"
Then God in his wisdom just says
"sorry old fella baby
you're gonna be fertilizer
for the chetstsnuts"
and turns the baby
into a piece of poo

#5

Brenda Browndinger
(when she was still inside)
sayed "Fuck off old... whoops   sorry!"
and that's why she smells funny
'cause God only half turned her

That's why we call her Liza
(ferta   liza)

I seen Brenda Browndinger
in the third cubicle
talkin' to a coming out poo...
she was yellin'
"APOLOGIZE
 APOLOGIZE
 AND YOU CAN GET TO BE A BABY!"
Then I heard a plop
and then she started cryin'

Poor Brenda

So I gived her
one of Toby's kittens

#6

Cunt is a bad word
see you and Ti na
not as bad as
If you see Kay
God's hair got ripped off 'cause
ya know 'cause
His mom's trap door was too small
God is bald as a bill yard
Hey
He likes to snuggle down in women's crotches at
night and imagines He's got hair again
That's one way baby's get born
the dust of heaven floats up inside ya

When I'm big
I'm gonna cut the hair on my
see you and Ti na
I don't want God
turning my baby into poo
'cause it swears

OR

imagine this

On God's birthday
Easter Sunday Night
I got a big hunk o' fur with glue on it

God comes for a snuggle
and wham!
I push the hunk of fur on his bald head

He gets up
looks in the mirror
says "Bless you my child
for I am whole again
and warm too."

Then Him and me get married
and I am the queen of heaven

#6b

When I become the queen of heaven
I'n gointa redesign it
a little

Like I'm gointa get more trees up there
for all the squirrels that Toby kills
and when God's in a frenzy
turning rude babies into poo
I'm gointa say "Hey old fella,
lighten up
Here's some apple crisp I made
outa the Tree o' Knowlege."

#9

Never look into a cat's eyes
for longer than ten seconds,
otherwise you lose your mind
The cat can mesmer you
and purr your brain out
into a jungle and you think
you're swinging from trees
but instead you're just at school
or at dinner and everyone thinks
"that kid is crazy."

That's what happened to Alistair,
that's why he's so nuts
but nobody knows
the cure is to eat cat food
and to live outside
for a week.
But nobody will let him do that

Poor fools,
they could have had
a normal little boy

The Hedge

#5

Melanie says flowers
were the first ones
to think of doing it

The amoebas
just split themselves

Flowers got uppity
They wanted to be pretty
They wanted to smell good
They sent messages to each other
like love letters
only made of dust
on the legs of bees

#22

There are brown fairies
and green ones

The green ones speak French
and turn themselves into cakes and frogs
The brown ones speak English
and do swears
and turn themselves into dog turds and soup

If you kiss a frog
it gets to be a prince
but it's always a fairy in it's brain

If you kiss a dog poo
you get a goblin
which is more fun
because they live in secret mountains
and have parties all the time

They steal children to do their cooking
because they eat mud pies
and kids are the best
at making those

#2

The belly button is wrinkly
because that's where our mouths used to be
before we got heads
and our arms were our ears
and we could fly

We can't fly now
because our heads are too heavy
and we need our hands
for making houses

We used to live in trees
like birds

#1006

Lilllian and I lie on our backs
in the garden
and look up at the sun
through the petals

Then we put them on our lips and eyelids
and stick out our tongues
waiting for a bee to land on the tip

if we swallow the bee
it will sting our heart
and a boy will love us

If we don't
we will be pregnant with flowers
and God will love us

*

ever seen a bee dance,
Lillian?

watch closely
they dance your dreams

they untangle your mind
so you can be a fortune teller

Music comes from dinosaur voices
locked in stones
and stored on the planet of sound

*

Bee's bums are filled with angel teeth
that's why they buzz

angel's teeth grinding
pollen into sound

*

Bees take their stripes off at night
and the stripes go whirling through the air
lassoing love talk

What d'you think a tornado is, Lillian?
bee stripes
on a rampage
for love

b1

Your rib cage, Lillian,
is to keep your heart
from flying out of your body
to perch on trees
'cause all hearts used to be birds

They get into your body
through your mother's mouth
on Thanksgiving and Christmas
when the wishbone cracks
That's why babies warble and stuff

Once a baby got two birds by mistake
and they porked each other
and the baby was filled with little birds
and they flew her round and round
and up to the sun
where she got cooked
and fell to earth
as a omlette

That's how Moses and them
got through the desert
when they were starving

b2

One baby got a pteranodon
and swallowed the moon
and exploded

That's the stars

There used to be two moons
headlights of the nightmobile
now there's only one

That's why the earth spins in circles
the nightmobile is doing wheelies
on the frozen sky
with only one headlight
and the earth has to dodge it

63

If you put a spider
on your tongue
the bird will crawl
up your windpipe
and tell you
ghost stories

b4

when babies turn into kids
the bird turns into a drum
that's why we like dancin'

And when you get old
the drum turns into a clock
saying get going
'cause soon
you'll die

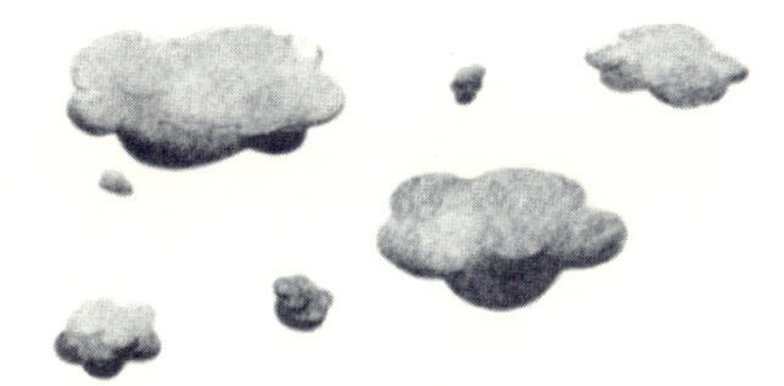

Hospital

What's a bone?

A space ship
from the planet Gonzo
planted neath your skin
to do the bidding
of the extraterrestrials

Before the space people came
we used to be piles of skin
that got around by wind
like kites

We were happier then
'cause we got to do more
lyin' around
and we could fly

#29

a scar...

what is it?

A zipper of skin
made by the goblin king

Anyone with a scar
has at least 5 – maybe 10
goblins livin' inside them

That's why criminals
got 'em all over
their face

Goblins
close to the brain

#30

Yer bum crack is a scar

If you don't poo
at least one time a day
you get a build up of goblins
and the doctor has to open you up

That's why doctors wear masks
so no goblins jump into their mouths

#308

Your bum crack
is the safest piggy bank
That's why bankers
stand up so straight
and clutch their bums together

So all that money doesn't
fall into the street

PING!... Every time
you hear that

a banker
let one go

#48

My knee is skinned
you know what that means,
eh Lillian?

It means that the goblins are on my side
That they wanted to see
underneath my skin
to see if I wasn't really a tree or something
or a robot

Then if I bled
which I did!
they would get me in their club
So now I'm just waiting
for them to call me

After I go to their meeting
at the stroke of midnight,
Lillian
I'll tell you all about it

Can I borrow
your roller blades?

#208

when ya die
the angels frizby
their halos down to the grave

what do you think
poor little sick girl?

The minute they hit dirt
they morphrodite into worms
and gobble you down

Then WHOOPEE
Back up to heaven

#12

Brenda Carbosier has hairy nostrils
so the nose fairies
could cluster in there
and keep warm
waiting for her to eat
her pumpkin pie

She has the best food

And then at night
they'd lower themselves down
like Rapunzel
and eat the crumbs off her lips.

Tonight
let's put some gravy in your nose
for the nose fairies

Then they'll make sure
the operation
goes OK

Jill

Jill #2

Jack and Jill
went up the hill
Jack was the devil
They both came
tumbling down but
God caught Jill and
put her up inta heaven

It's cleaner up there
But she still pines for
the good old days

Jill #1

Brenda Impry is a cunt on two legs
that's why she's so hairy and wet
and why her mouth is on sideways
cause she wouldn't do her work
so God said "Ok Brenda Impry,
you are now a cunt
and all you have to do is lie around
and flap your lips"
But then one day
when Brenda was flapping
she lifted right off – she flew
She flew up to heaven
and God said "Hey, what's that"
It was Brenda Impry
and God said, "Shoot her down,Gabriel"
and Gabriel dragged out his dong
and fired pearls at her
and the pearls caught in her hair
and one went inside her and got real big
and then her water broke inside her
and the ocean fell out of Brenda Impry
and God told his son Jesus
to make fish so they could spy on the water
God said "Dip the sun in the water
and heat it up,"

so they – the angels –
lowered the sun into the sea
and it sizzled and the sea got warm and bubbly
and fish stuck to the sun
and God sucked off the fish
and they said "The water whispers
secrets to the moon"
and God said "What secrets?"
and the fish said
"Secrets about night
and what happened to your wife."

Jill #4

God's wife Jill
lives on the second shelf of paradise
in a box of feathers
She keeps her tongue
in a crystal bowl
and wears cat feet for silence
She can light matches with her eyes
That's why God keeps her there
so she doesn't set heaven on fire

Jill #6

Leave a feather on a rock
for Jill, Lillian
and she'll fly you up to the sun
It's fun
but if you hit the sun
you turn into a raisin

That's what I'm eating
right now –
a fried-up kid
covered in chocolate

#7

Some say
There is no devil anymore
'cause he turned into God
after he fell in love
with Jill and her wild ways

or vice versa

OR some say

God and Jill
useta live on a island and
were part horse but then
Jill ate a apple with a worm in it,
turned into a morphrodite and
took over
God cried so hard he turned into
a rain cloud and that's why
he lives in heaven

Jill #8

Gram is friends with Jill...
She and Jill go to the planet Venus
made of peacocks
and they do peacock hunts

Their fingernails
whiz thru the air
like arrows

Gram hauls those dead old peacocks home
and that's what we eat
at Christmas

Once they made a boo boo
and shot down a angel

Jill hid in her box
for seven years
and wove a suit of fish scales
which she gave to the angel's mom

The mom liked it
but it sure stunk

Jill #10

God loves Jill
but he's scared of her
bleeds on his angels

They cost a lot
to dry clean

Jill #9

God's wife Jill
comes from the planet Oona
which is a onion

On the planet Oona
all the girls cry and cry
cause they scratch it
with their cat feet
then the tears make fish
for them to eat
and a ocean
for them to swim in

#22

In the Garden of Eden,
Lillian
there was a onion tree
God's wife Jill
bit a onion
and cried and cried

All the snakes
in the Garden of Eden
were drowning
so Jill made magic
and gave them
water wings
and that's a fish

Jill#11

God said
every Friday
we eat swimming snakes
and Jill cut off her tongue
and put it in a crystal bowl
She was sad

Jill#12

The tongue was called John
she fed it peacock bits
and it got pretty

One day John escaped
and crawled into God's strawberry patch
where the ghost Jesus was wandering
John sang this song
"Fish don't hiss
'cause there's water in their mouths"
Jesus fell in love with John
and John swallowed him
then and there

Jill #13

Jill knew Jesus was in her tongue
She could sense it
so she sent it to school to get a education
"Teach it about deserts"
she said to Gram who was the teacher
"and teach it to phone home"

Gram taught the tongue Jesus all she knew
and when June came
Gram rubbed it with cinnamon

It sprouted arms and legs and a head
and that was Adam
and then Jill came to pick up her weird boy
and saw this new boy and she said
"Well Gram, I guess you did your best"
and Gram said "thanks Jill"
and they all went to Oona
and drank onion juice
and cried

Jill #14

One day, Lillian
a crow came flying
with a sunflower in her beak
and plonked it
in Jill's crystal bowl

God was just frying up
some swimming snakes

Jill and Gram were doing signals to earth
telling the angels
which countries to put clouds on

The sunflower seed went *ping*
and the sound made everyone jiggle

When they jiggled their ears fell off
and floated down to earth
and landed in the ground
and up grew the six Eves

They could hear every whisper
but they couldn't speak a word
and poor old Adam, all he could do
was talk but never hear...

...so they loved each other.

The End

Thanks to:

The Canada Council Explorations Program, and
The Ontario Arts Council

and

rick, the agnews, the moores, darren, denise, death, cat, heather, victor, geoffry, rick/simon, hilary, phil, marina, jane, pages, keen communications, the women's bookstore, the women's press, beverly, tasha, chip, kate, the jessies, the burimas, mrs. jetzki, melissa, alexis, the woolfs, damian, md wing, ralph, michael, mike, janette, janet, raymon, roz, burg, bill, bucky, gypsy, piper, the goodwill of joanne and the wild zone

Typeset in Providence and printed at Coach House Printing on bpNichol Lane, 1999.

Edited by Victor Coleman and Darren Wershler-Henry

To read the online version of this text and other titles from Coach House Books, or to order any of out titles,
visit our website:

www.chbooks.com

To add your name to our e-mailing list, write:

mail@chbooks.com

Toll-free:

1 800 367 6360

Conventional mail:

Coach House Books
401 Huron (rear) on bpNichol Lane
Toronto, Ontario M5S 2G5